Writer Caroline Bretherton

Editor Ann Barton

Senior Designer Sonia Moore

Project Art Editor Vicky Read

Photography Art Direction Nigel Wright

Photography Rob Streeter

Jacket Designer Nicola Powling

Associate Publisher Billy Fields

Publisher Mike Sanders

First American Edition, 2017
Published in the United States by
DK Publishing
6081 E. 82nd Street,
Indianapolis, Indiana 46250

Published in the United States
by Dorling Kindersley Limited.

A catalog record for this book is available from
the Library of Congress.
ISBN: 978-1-4654-6271-8

DK books are available at special discounts
when purchased in bulk for sales promotions,
premiums, fund-raising, or educational use. For
details, contact: DK Publishing Special Markets,
345 Hudson Street, New York, New York 10014
or SpecialSales@dk.com.

Printed and bound in China

All images © Dorling Kindersley Limited
For further information see: www.dkimages.com

A WORLD OF IDEAS:
SEE ALL THERE IS TO KNOW

www.dk.com

Sprouted!
SEEDS, GRAINS & BEANS

CONTENTS

Pick a recipe

SUPER GREEN SMOOTHIE
Page 30

RAW ENERGY BARS
Page 40

SPROUTED SUMMER
ROLLS
Page 50

SPROUTED BEAN
BURGERS
Page 60

*Mix it up! Beans
to sprout together 48*

*Mix it up!
Grains to sprout
together 58*

*Mix it up!
Seeds to sprout
together 38*

6

SPICED CARROT
MUFFINS
Page 32

BUCKWHEAT PORRIDGE
Page 34

EMMER BREAKFAST
BOWL
Page 35

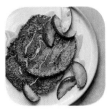

WHOLE WHEAT
PANCAKES
Page 36

TABBOULEH
Page 42

SPROUTED GRAIN SALAD
Page 43

AVOCADO TOASTS
Page 44

SAVORY CABBAGE
PANCAKES
Page 46

WHITE BEAN SOUP
Page 52

ADZUKI BEAN CURRY
Page 53

ASIAN STYLE SALAD
Page 54

BROWN RICE
SUSHI BOWL
Page 56

SPROUTED HUMMUS
Page 62

BLACK BEAN
QUESADILLA
Page 63

VEGETABLE STIR-FRY
Page 64

ROOT VEGETABLE STEW
Page 66

WHAT ARE **SPROUTS?**

Sprouts are immature plants—the little shoots that begin to grow when a seed germinates. They're healthy, delicious, and easy to grow at home.

HOW A SEED SPROUTS

The sprouts we eat come from seeds that have been soaked in water, which jump-starts the germination process. Within a dormant seed is everything a plant needs to grow. Once the seed has been soaked, compounds that protect against early germination are neutralized and chemical changes begin to occur. Enzymes are produced to allow the growing sprout to access the nutrients within the seed. As the developing sprout grows, it is nourished by complex carbohydrates and proteins, which are broken down into simple sugars and amino acids. With these nutrients available, the cells multiply quickly, producing a little sprout in just a few days.

Nutrients within the bean are protected by the hard outer shell

The first part of the plant to emerge is the primary root

Dry bean   **Soaked bean**   **1 day later**   **2 days later**   **3 days later**

TEXTURES AND FLAVORS

From delicate tendrils to robust shoots, sprouts are as varied as the seeds from which they come. Many sprouts reflect the flavors of the full-grown plant, such as spicy radish sprouts and sweet, mild cabbage sprouts. Harvest your sprouts right after they emerge or let them grow long for more texture.

Sprouted seeds tend to be thin and delicate.

Sprouted legumes produce hearty, crunchy sprouts.

Sprouted grains have a chewy texture when cooked.

SOAKING VS. SPROUTING

Soaking is the first step in the sprouting process, but you can soak without sprouting, too. An overnight soak will impart some of the nutritional benefits of sprouting, making the seed, grain, bean, or nut more digestible and the nutrients within more bio-available.

Chickpeas double in size after an overnight soak

SOAKED NUTS

Most nuts can be soaked but will not sprout. If you choose to soak your nuts, choose raw, unsalted varieties. Soaked nuts become plump and take on a creamy texture.

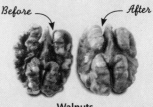

Before — *After*

Walnuts

Before — *After*

Cashews

9

WHY ARE **SPROUTS SUPER?**

There's a lot to love about these little seedlings. In just a few days, you can transform a handful of seeds into an indoor garden, ready to add tasty texture and loads of nutrients to just about any dish.

Sprouts are an easy way to grow fresh food indoors at any time of year. A sprouting jar and the seeds, beans, or grains of your choice are all you need to get started growing sprouts at home. With flavors ranging from sweet to spicy, there's something to please every palate and enhance any meal.

Within every seed, there are vital nutrients just waiting to be unlocked. The process of soaking and sprouting deactivates anti-nutrients in seeds, such as phytic acid. This compound protects against early germination, but also binds to essential minerals such as calcium,

iron, and zinc, and prevents them from being absorbed in the digestive tract. When the sprout begins to grow, it activates phytase, an enzyme that breaks the bond between the phytic acid and the minerals, making them more bioavailable. Germination also triggers chemical changes that actually boost the levels of key nutrients such as amino acids, vitamin C, vitamin A, and some B vitamins. The difference in the vitamin content between sprouted grains and beans and their non-sprouted counterparts can be impressive, from only trace amounts in the dry seed to nutritionally significant levels in the sprouts.

"Sprouting increases vitamin C in chickpeas by 300 percent"

Grains, beans, and seeds become more digestible and better for you. The enzymes activated by sprouting aid digestion in a variety of ways. In addition to neutralizing phytic acid, which can be irritating to the gut, enzymes act as catalysts to break down the complex carbohydrates and plant protein within the seed into more easily digested simple sugars and amino acids. This makes the protein more bioavailable and reduces some of the negative effects of eating beans and whole grains, such as bloating and gas. Sprouting also promotes the growth of vital digestive enzymes that help to maintain gut health. Taken together, the health benefits of sprouts make them a true superfood.

A vegetable garden you can grow indoors

THE **BEST BEANS** TO SPROUT

1. *Mung beans*
A staple in Chinese cuisine, mung beans produce thick white shoots with a mild flavor. Rinse frequently and sprout in a dark environment for best results. Enjoy raw or cooked.

2. *Cannellini beans*
Cannellini beans, also known as white kidney beans, have a mild flavor and hold their shape well when cooked, making them a good choice for soups and stews. Sprouted cannellini beans should not be eaten raw.

3. *Navy beans*
This dense and meaty white bean is the classic choice for baked beans and other braised dishes. Sprouted navy beans should not be eaten raw, but can be steamed for a fresh flavor.

4. *Chickpeas*
Hearty and slightly sweet, sprouted chickpeas pair well with strong spices, such as curry and cumin. Add them to stews, roast them for snacking, or make a creamy, raw hummus.

Cut down the cooking time and boost the nutrition of your favorite bean, pea, and lentil dishes by sprouting your legumes first. Note that some sprouted beans are not suitable for eating raw.

5. Peas
Most varieties of whole, dried peas can be sprouted. Just-sprouted peas are sturdy enough to use in cooked dishes, while longer pea shoots are best enjoyed raw in salads or as a garnish.

6. Black beans
When cooked, sprouted black beans develop a creamy texture that's perfect for blending or mashing. Black beans sprout best in cooler temperatures and should not be eaten raw.

7. Lentils
Lentils are available in a rainbow of colors and are easy to sprout. Raw sprouted lentils make a crunchy, fresh addition to salads, while cooked sprouted lentils can be used for bean burgers, soups, and casseroles.

8. Adzuki beans
These dark red beans are full of soluble fiber and have a low glycemic index. Eat the crisp, slightly sweet sprouts raw, or cook the just-sprouted beans in chilis and curries.

THE **BEST SEEDS** TO SPROUT

Sproutable seeds come in a wide range of sizes and colors, and produce sprouts that are nearly as varied. These are some of the most easily sourced and delicious seeds for sprouting.

1. Pumpkin

With their nutty flavor and rich, buttery texture, sprouted pumpkin seeds make a satisfying snack on their own, or a crunchy addition to baked goods. Considered a soak rather than a true sprout, pumpkin seeds are ready when a tiny shoot appears at the tip.

2. Sunflower

Sunflower seeds are quick to sprout and have a mild crunch. They can be eaten on their own or used to add flavor and texture to salads and baked goods. A shorter sprout time (1–2 days) is best for cooked applications.

3. Broccoli

Broccoli sprouts are particularly rich in antioxidants and have a slightly peppery, cabbage-like flavor. The white fuzz that appears on the sprout are root hairs, not mold.

4. Red clover

This easy-to-grow, leafy sprout has a pleasant, mildly sweet flavor. Similar to alfalfa, it turns green when exposed to sunlight. Red clover sprouts are best for salads, sandwiches, or juicing.

5. Quinoa

Tiny sprouted quinoa seeds have a light texture and pleasing crunch. With all nine essential amino acids, quinoa sprouts provide a complete protein and can be eaten raw or lightly cooked.

6. Sesame

Small and tender, sprouted sesame seeds make a delicious nutty topping for a wide variety of dishes. Sprinkle them on stir-fries and salads, or scatter them over a loaf of sprouted bread for texture. Both black and white varieties are suitable for sprouting.

7. Mustard

Like mustard greens, sprouted mustard seeds have a hot, spicy flavor. There are several varieties, including Oriental, Mizuna, and brown. Mustard seeds sprout best when mixed with other seeds.

8. Alfalfa

Mild and easy to grow, alfalfa is one of the most familiar sprout varieties. The delicate sprouts naturally clump together as they grow, creating a crisp tangle. To turn the leaves green, set your sprouter in the sun for a few hours on the last day of sprouting.

9. Radish

Many varieties of radish seeds can be used for sprouting, from Daikon to China Rose. Depending on the variety, the flavor can range from mildly hot to seriously spicy. Use them whenever you want a bit of heat.

THE **BEST GRAINS** TO SPROUT

2

4

1

5

3

1. Oats

The chewy texture and sweet flavor of sprouted oats are perfect for breakfast. Choose whole, hulless oats, which are grown without a hull. Rolled oats and steel cut oats are not suitable for sprouting.

2. Brown rice

Sprouted brown rice cooks more quickly than regular brown rice, and has a more delicate texture and a slightly sweeter flavor.

3. Buckwheat groats

Buckwheat groats sprout quickly and have a nutty flavor and tender texture. Despite its name, buckwheat is not wheat-derived and is a delicious gluten-free alternative to other grains.

4. Spelt

Spelt is a variety of hulled wheat with a mild flavor that lends itself to grain salads and baking. Short sprouts are best for grinding into flour.

5. Millet

These tiny, round seeds sprout quickly and have a mild crunch. Their small size and bright color make them a

Sprouting is a wonderful way to enjoy whole grains without digestion issues. For extended shelf life, dry just-sprouted grains and store in the freezer for later use, or grind into flour.

unique addition to whole-grain bread or breakfast porridge blends.

6. Barley
Chewy and slightly less sweet than other wheat-derived grains, sprouted barley is excellent for porridges and grain salad. Seek out hulless varieties (those grown without a hull) for sprouting.

7. Wheat berries
Available in white and red varieties, wheat berries sprout quickly and produce a sweet, chewy sprout perfect for grinding into flour or making grain salad.

8. Emmer
Like spelt, emmer is an ancient variety of hulled wheat that is hearty and chewy. Try sprouted emmer in grain salads, cereals, casseroles, or stews.

9. Rye
Easy-to-sprout and versatile, sprouted rye has less gluten than sprouted wheat, and unlike other grains, the enzymes activated during sprouting can withstand the heat of baking.

SOAK AND SPROUT GUIDE

Red clover

Adzuki beans

Buckwheat groats

SEEDS	SOAK
ALFALFA	6–10 hrs
BROCCOLI	8–10 hrs
MUSTARD	6–12 hrs
PUMPKIN	2–6 hrs
QUINOA	30 mins–1 hr
RADISH	6–12 hrs
RED CLOVER	8–10 hrs
SESAME	2–8 hrs
SUNFLOWER	1–3 hrs

BEANS	
ADZUKI BEANS	8–10 hrs
BLACK BEANS	8–12 hrs
CANNELLINI BEANS	8–12 hrs
CHICKPEAS	8–12 hrs
LENTILS	8–12 hrs
MUNG BEANS	6–12 hrs
NAVY BEANS	8–10 hrs
WHOLE PEAS	4–8 hrs

GRAINS	
BARLEY	6–12 hrs
BROWN RICE	4–24 hrs
BUCKWHEAT GROATS	30 mins–1 hr
EMMER	4–12 hrs
MILLET	6–10 hrs
OATS	1–4 hrs
RYE	6–12 hrs
SPELT	4–8 hrs
WHEAT BERRIES	4–12 hrs

Rinse all sprouts twice each day while sprouting. The times and yields given are estimates and may vary based on conditions.

SPROUT	DRY MEASURE	YIELD
4–6 days	1 tbsp (6g)	3–4 cups (50g)
3–6 days	1 tbsp (6g)	3–4 cups (50g)
3–6 days	1 tbsp (6g)	3–4 cups (50g)
1–3 days	½ cup (75g)	¾ cup (115g)
1–2 days	½ cup (85g)	¾ cup (140g)
3–6 days	1 tbsp (6g)	3–4 cups (50g)
4–6 days	1 tbsp (6g)	3–4 cups (50g)
1–3 days	1 tbsp (9g)	½ cup (75g)
1–2 days	¼ cup (40g)	⅓ cup (60g)
2–4 days	½ cup (104g)	2 cups (200g)
2–4 days	½ cup (90g)	2 cups (200g)
2–4 days	½ cup (96g)	2 cups (200g)
2–4 days	½ cup (100g)	2 cups (200g)
2–3 days	½ cup (100g)	2½ cups (250g)
2–5 days	½ cup (108g)	2½ cups (250g)
2–4 days	½ cup (96g)	2 cups (200g)
2–3 days	½ cup (100g)	2½ cups (250g)
2–3 days	½ cup (90g)	¾ cup (140g)
2–4 days	½ cup (100g)	¾ cup (140g)
1–3 days	½ cup (85g)	¾ cup (140g)
2–3 days	½ cup (90g)	¾ cup (140g)
1–3 days	½ cup (110g)	¾ cup (140g)
1–3 days	½ cup (40g)	¾ cup (60g)
2–3 days	½ cup (90g)	¾ cup (140g)
2–3 days	½ cup (90g)	¾ cup (140g)
2–3 days	½ cup (90g)	¾ cup (140g)

WHAT YOU NEED
TO GET STARTED

All sprouts need to grow is a moist environment with adequate airflow. You can make your own sprouting set up, or purchase containers specifically designed for home sprouting.

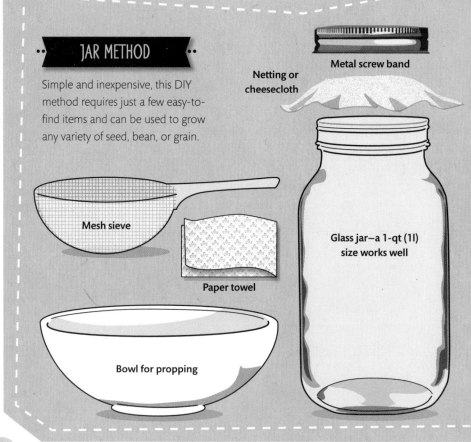

JAR METHOD

Simple and inexpensive, this DIY method requires just a few easy-to-find items and can be used to grow any variety of seed, bean, or grain.

Metal screw band

Netting or cheesecloth

Mesh sieve

Paper towel

Glass jar—a 1-qt (1l) size works well

Bowl for propping

Purchase special sprouting lids, or use a rubber band to hold netting in place

TRAY METHOD

Often available in stackable formats, sprouting trays are a reliable way to grow sprouts and offer the easiest rinsing option. Sprouting trays come in a variety of styles, but are usually made of plastic with a perforated bottom to allow for easy draining. Most varieties of sprouts do well in trays.

Stackable trays allow you to sprout multiple seed varieties at once

Use a tea towel for propping instead of a bowl

You can use materials other than those shown to set up your sprouting jar, as long as the lid provides adequate drainage and the base of the jar is elevated.

BAG METHOD

Lightweight, durable, and portable, hemp sprouting bags are a convenient method for growing most varieties of sprouts, particularly beans and grains. Rinsing is easy; you simply run water through the bag and then hang it up or set it in a dish rack to drain.

Hemp is a breathable fabric that allows airflow for sprouting

SAFE SPROUTING

The warm, moist environment sprouts need to thrive is the same environment bacteria likes, too. Following a few simple guidelines will keep your sprouts tasty and safe.

START WITH THE RIGHT SEEDS

The best way to eliminate the risk of contamination is by choosing certified organic seeds that are intended for sprouting. These seeds are most often found through online retailers or health food stores. Avoid conventionally grown seeds and those intended for planting.

CLEAN YOUR EQUIPMENT

Any equipment used for sprouting should be thoroughly cleaned before use. At the very least, wash equipment with hot, soapy water and air dry. You may also choose to sanitize your equipment by running it through the sanitize cycle on your dishwasher or by soaking it in a dilute bleach solution. Use ½ cup bleach per gallon of water, soak equipment for 5 minutes, rinse well, and air dry.

CLEAN YOUR SEEDS

As an extra precaution, you can sanitize your seeds prior to sprouting. In a saucepan, heat 3% hydrogen peroxide to 140°F (60°C). Place your seeds in a fine mesh sieve and lower into the hydrogen peroxide solution until they are completely submerged. Let the seeds soak for 5 minutes, swirling occasionally. Monitor the temperature while seeds soak, maintaining 140°F (60°C). Then rinse seeds under filtered, room-temperature water.

Due to the risk of contamination, children, pregnant women, and those with weakened immune systems should avoid eating raw sprouts.

5 steps for success

- **Sanitize** your equipment.

- Handle sprouts and sprouting equipment with **clean hands**.

- Check sprouts when rinsing and **drain thoroughly**.

- Let sprouts **air dry** before storing. (Sprouts should feel dry to the touch.)

- Refrigerate in an **airtight container** for up to five days.

KEEP SPROUTS HAPPY

Sprouts are susceptible to spoilage if inadequately drained or improperly stored. Each time you rinse, check your sprouts for signs of mold. The stems should be white or cream colored. Give your sprouts a sniff, too. Healthy sprouts smell fresh, not moldy. Drain sprouts very thoroughly after rinsing. If any sprouts look questionable, discard the batch.

HOW TO **SPROUT**

This simple method is a quick way to start sprouting, and it works well for most varieties of seeds, grains, and beans. For best results, sanitize your seeds and equipment before you begin.

SPROUT TIP

Be sure to drain thoroughly! Inadequate drainage is the most common cause of moldy or contaminated sprouts.

Fill halfway or more

A bowl works well as a stand

1. SOAK

Place seeds, grains, or beans in jar. Add filtered water to fill jar at least halfway. Cover with sprouting lid. Soak as directed, depending on variety (see pages 18–19).

2. DRAIN AND RINSE

Drain the soaking water. Remove the sprouting lid and rinse the seeds, grains, or beans with filtered water, swirling gently. Replace the lid and drain again.

3. SPROUT

In a well-ventilated spot, away from direct sunlight, place the jar on its side. Prop up the base so that water can drain. Place paper towel under the mouth of the jar to absorb excess water.

Mix it up!

Seeds, grains, and beans with similar sprouting times can be sprouted together in the same jar.

Sprout a mix of seeds for a variety of flavors

Try mixing lentils, mung beans, chickpeas, and adzuki beans for a rainbow of colors and textures. Or blend clover, radish, alfalfa, and mustard for a mildly sweet mix with peppery undertones.

4. RINSE AND DRAIN

At least twice a day, add filtered water to the jar and swirl to rinse. Drain thoroughly after rinsing and return jar to the sprouting position with the base elevated.

5. WATCH AND WAIT

Depending on the variety, your seeds, grains, or beans will begin to sprout in 1–3 days. The emerging sprout will look like a little tail coming out of the seed, bean, or grain.

6. HARVEST

When ready to eat, rinse and drain a final time and remove from sprouting jar. Spread on a paper towel to remove all excess moisture. Sprouts can be refrigerated in an airtight container for up to 5 days.

DRYING SPROUTS
FOR FLOUR

Making sprouted flour is an easy way to get even more from your sprouted grains. To maintain beneficial enzyme activity, use the air drying or dehydrating method.

AIR DRYING

Spread your sprouted grains in a single layer on a baking sheet and cover with cheesecloth to deter fruit flies. Place the baking sheet in a dry, well-ventilated spot. Turn the grains every few hours to ensure even drying. Air drying takes 18 to 48 hours, depending on temperature and humidity.

Dry multiple varieties of sprouts at once in a dehydrator

Cover your sprouts with a breathable fabric while drying

USING A DEHYDRATOR

Dehydrators are the easiest and most reliable way to achieve dried sprouts. You may need to line the dehydrator trays with non-stick dehydrator sheets to prevent small grains from slipping through the holes. Grains will take about 12 to 18 hours to dry in a dehydrator.

DRYING IN THE OVEN

This method dries grains quickly, but will decrease the enzymes activated by sprouting. Preheat the oven to 150°F (65°C), or the lowest temperature possible. Spread your sprouted grains in a single layer on a baking sheet and place in the oven. Drying will take 6 to 10 hours, depending on the moisture content of your grain.

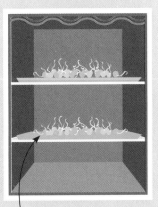

Turn your sprouted grain with a spatula every hour or so to ensure even drying

WHAT GRAINS TO CHOOSE?

Any sprouted grain can be dried and ground into flour. Flour made from sprouted wheat varieties can be used in place of regular wheat flour. When sprouting grain for flour, it's best to dry just after the sprout begins to emerge.

Sprouted wheat berries

TESTING FOR DRYNESS

Grain that has not fully dried can begin to mold. Test your grain for dryness by weighing it before sprouting and again after sprouting and drying. The dried, sprouted grain should be about the same weight as the dry grain before sprouting.

Dried wheat berries

GRINDING YOUR FLOUR

Grind your dried sprouted grain into flour using a flour mill or high-powered blender. Place the grain in the mill and process until it is finely ground and no large pieces remain. Store sprouted flour in an airtight container in the freezer for up to 12 months.

Wheat berry flour

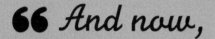 **"And now,**

 **20 DELICIOUS, SPROUTED recipes for YOU! "**

Look out for the gluten-free recipes.

Gluten Free

With its silky texture and tangy, tropical flavor, this nutrient-rich superfood smoothie is a healthy and refreshing way to start your day.

SUPER GREEN SMOOTHIE
with KALE, SPROUTS, *and* MANGO

SERVES 2

1 cup loosely packed de-ribbed and shredded kale

1 cup loosely packed alfalfa sprouts

½ cup loosely packed baby spinach

½ small ripe avocado, roughly chopped

½ heaped cup frozen mango chunks

1 tbsp sprouted sunflower seeds

1 tbsp sprouted pumpkin seeds

1 cup coconut water

½ cup apple juice

PREP 5 MINUTES

1 Place all the ingredients in a high-powered blender or smoothie maker and blend until completely smooth.

2 Pour into two glasses and drink immediately.

SPROUT SWAP
Alfalfa can be replaced with any mild-flavored sprout, such as red clover.

Sprouting time...

Alfalfa seeds
Soak 8-12 hours
Sprout 5-6 days

Pumpkin and sunflower seeds
Soak 2-3 hours
Sprout 1 day

Gluten Free

These wholesome muffins are made extra moist with grated carrot and flavored with warming spices. Sprouted pumpkin seeds add a nutty crunch.

SPICED CARROT MUFFINS
with APRICOTS *and* SPROUTED PUMPKIN SEEDS

MAKES 12

PREP 10 MINUTES   **COOK** 15-20 MINUTES

1 cup white whole wheat flour

1 tsp baking powder

½ tsp baking soda

1 tsp cinnamon

¼ tsp ground nutmeg

¼ tsp ground ginger

⅓ cup light brown sugar

⅓ cup finely diced
dried apricots + extra
for topping

¼ cup sprouted pumpkin seeds
+ extra for topping

1 large egg

¾ cup whole milk

¼ cup coconut oil, liquefied
and cooled

½ cup packed finely grated carrot

1 Preheat the oven to 425°F (210°C) and line a 12-hole muffin tin with paper baking cups. In a large bowl, use a balloon whisk to whisk together flour, baking powder, baking soda, cinnamon, nutmeg, ginger, and brown sugar. Add the dried apricot and pumpkin seeds and mix until well combined.

2 In a medium bowl, whisk together the egg, milk, and coconut oil until well combined.

3 Make a well in the center of the dry ingredients and pour in the liquid ingredients. Stir until just combined, and then gently fold in the grated carrot.

4 Divide the mixture evenly among the baking cups and sprinkle with additional pumpkin seeds and diced apricot. Bake for 15–20 minutes, until muffins are well risen and golden brown.

5 Allow the muffins to cool in the tin for at least 5 minutes before transferring them to a wire rack to cool completely. Like most muffins, these are best eaten the day they are made.

Sprouting time... } **Pumpkin seeds**
Soak 2-3 hours
Sprout 1 day

The warm flavors of cinnamon and maple complement the nuttiness of sprouted and dried buckwheat in this hearty breakfast porridge.

BUCKWHEAT PORRIDGE
with MAPLE and TOASTED HAZELNUTS

SERVES 1

PREP 10 MINUTES   **COOK** 15–20 MINUTES

¼ cup raw hazelnuts

½ cup sprouted and dried buckwheat (see p26)

¾ cup almond milk

pinch of fine sea salt

1 small piece of cinnamon stick

maple syrup, to serve

1 Preheat the oven to 350°F (175°C). Spread hazelnuts on a baking sheet and place on the top rack of the oven. Bake for 5–7 minutes, until golden brown. Allow them to cool, then rub them in a clean kitchen towel to remove the skins, roughly chop, and set aside.

2 Put the buckwheat in a small heavy-bottomed saucepan. Add the almond milk, salt, and cinnamon stick and bring to a boil. Reduce to a simmer and cook for 10–12 minutes, stirring occasionally, until the buckwheat is plump and soft, adding more almond milk if needed to maintain a creamy consistency. Remove the cinnamon stick.

3 Place the porridge in a serving bowl and scatter some of the chopped hazelnuts on top (the rest can be stored in an airtight container for future use). Top with maple syrup to serve.

Gluten Free

Sprouting time... }

Buckwheat
Soak 30 minutes
Sprout 2 days

Caramelized blackberries and apple top this warming breakfast bowl,
which features emmer, a type of farro suitable for sprouting.

EMMER BREAKFAST BOWL
with APPLE *and* BLACKBERRY COMPOTE

SERVES 1

½ cup sprouted and dried
emmer (see p26)

1 cup milk

½ tbsp butter

½ small apple, peeled, cored,
and sliced into segments

handful of blackberries,
halved if large

1 tbsp raw sliced almonds

½ tsp light brown sugar

PREP 5 MINUTES   **COOK** 20-25 MINUTES

1 Crack the dried emmer by pulsing it in a high-powered blender with a grinding blade until it has broken up into large pieces.

2 Place the emmer and milk in a small heavy-bottomed saucepan and bring to a boil over medium heat. Reduce to a simmer and cook, covered, for 20–25 minutes, stirring occasionally, until it has softened and absorbed nearly all the milk.

3 Just before the emmer is ready, melt the butter in a small frying pan over medium heat. When it is sizzling, add the apple slices and fry them for 3 minutes, until they begin to soften.

4 Add the blackberries to the apples, and cook for another 2 minutes until the fruit has softened. Add the almonds and sugar and cook for a minute more until the sugar has dissolved.

5 Transfer the cooked emmer to a bowl and serve immediately with the apple and blackberry compote piled on top.

Sprouting time... } **Emmer**
Soak 8-12 hours
Sprout 2 days

Homemade sprouted wheat flour gives these pancakes a rustic texture and nutty flavor, while freshly grated apple adds sweetness and moisture.

WHOLE WHEAT PANCAKES
with APPLE *and* CINNAMON

MAKES 8

PREP 15 MINUTES   **COOK** 6 MINUTES

1 cup flour made from sprouted and dried wheat berries
(see p26)

1 tsp baking powder

1 tbsp sugar

½ tsp cinnamon

⅛ tsp fine sea salt

1 large egg

⅔ cup whole milk

1 tbsp butter, melted and cooled
+ extra for frying

1 medium apple, peeled, cored, and finely grated

TO SERVE

maple syrup

a few apple slices

lemon juice

1 In a large bowl, whisk together the sprouted wheat berry flour, baking powder, sugar, cinnamon, and salt. In a small bowl, beat together the egg and milk.

2 Make a well in the center of the dry ingredients, pour in the milk mixture, and whisk to combine. Once it is completely combined, add the cooled, melted butter and whisk again. Gently fold in the grated apple.

3 In a large non-stick frying pan, melt a little butter over medium heat. Spoon small amounts of batter into the hot pan, to create pancakes approximately 4 inches (10cm) across. Use the back of the spoon to smooth the tops of the pancakes.

4 Cook for 3 minutes over medium-low heat, until the pancakes look set around the edges. Carefully turn the pancakes and cook for another 2–3 minutes. Serve immediately with maple syrup or apple slices, pan-fried in butter and finished with lemon juice.

Sprouting time...

Wheat berries
Soak 8-12 hours
Sprout 1-2 days

Mix it up!
SEEDS to **SPROUT** TOGETHER

Mixing seeds with similar sprouting times is a wonderful way to create a custom blend of flavors. In this mix, sweet clover and alfalfa balance spicy mustard and radish for a delicious and nutrient-rich sandwich topping.

SOAK 8 HOURS   **SPROUT** 6 DAYS

Alfalfa
Like clover, alfalfa sprouts have a mild, grassy flavor. They also contain significant amounts of vitamin K, which is essential for building bones.

Mustard
Tiny mustard seeds produce a peppery sprout that are loaded with vitamins and nutrients including vitamins A, B6, and C, calcium, and iron.

Clover
Mild clover is the perfect counterpart to spicier radish and mustard. It is also a rich source of phytoestrogens, which can be a benefit to women's health.

Radish
Like full-grown radishes, radish sprouts are hot and spicy. They're also an excellent source of glucosinolates, chemical compounds that may help prevent cancer.

Mix and match the dried fruits and seeds in these wholesome energy bars as you prefer, but keep the quantities similar.

RAW ENERGY BARS
with DATES *and* SPROUTED BUCKWHEAT

MAKES 16

PREP 10 MINUTES, PLUS 4 HOURS TO CHILL

1 cup roughly chopped pitted Medjool dates

½ cup roughly chopped pitted prunes

½ cup raw hazelnuts

½ cup sprouted and dried buckwheat (see p26)

½ cup raw sliced almonds

½ cup unsweetened flaked coconut

⅓ cup roughly chopped dried cherries

¼ cup sprouted pumpkin seeds

¼ cup sprouted sunflower seeds

2 tbsp raw cacao powder

1 Put the dates and prunes in a heatproof bowl and cover with hot water. Let soak for 5 minutes. Put the hazelnuts in a food processor and pulse until they are broken up into pieces.

2 Drain the dates and prunes and loosely squeeze them dry, leaving them still damp. Place them in the food processor with the hazelnuts and add all the remaining ingredients.

3 Process the mixture until it is well combined, the nuts and seeds are in small pieces, and the mixture begins to form a ball. It will be very stiff, so you may need to scrape down the sides of the bowl and break it up occasionally with a spoon.

4 Turn out the mixture into a 9-inch (20cm) square baking pan, and use damp hands to push it into an even layer. Use the back of a large metal spoon, dampened, to even out the surface of the mixture, then chill for at least 3–4 hours.

5 Turn out the mixture onto a board and cut into 16 equally sized pieces. Wrap individually in wax paper and store in an airtight container in the refrigerator until needed.

Sprouting time... }

Buckwheat
Soak 30 minutes
Sprout 2 days

Pumpkin and sunflower seeds
Soak 2–3 hours
Sprout 1 day

"Fiber in buckwheat can reduce food cravings and support weight loss"

Gluten Free

Sprouted wheat berries give this tabbouleh a robust, chewy texture that is complemented by sharp, salty feta and a mix of fresh herbs.

TABBOULEH
with FETA *and* MINT

SERVES 4-6

2 cups dried sprouted wheat berries (see p26)

4 tbsp extra virgin olive oil

2 tbsp lemon juice

handful of flat-leaf parsley, finely chopped

handful of mint, finely chopped

handful of dill, finely chopped

salt and freshly ground pepper

1 bunch scallions, trimmed and finely chopped

6-in (15cm) segment English cucumber, deseeded and finely diced

12 cherry tomatoes, quartered

½ cup crumbled feta cheese

PREP 10 MINUTES   **COOK** 20-25 MINUTES

1 Put the wheat berries into a medium heavy-bottomed saucepan and cover with 2 inches (5cm) cold water. Bring to a boil, then reduce to a simmer and cook, uncovered, for 20–25 minutes until they are soft. Drain them well and refresh under cold water before allowing them to cool.

2 Once cool, put the cooked wheat berries into a large bowl and add the olive oil, lemon juice, and chopped herbs. Season well with salt and pepper and toss to combine. Add the scallions, cucumber, and tomatoes and toss again. Finally, add the feta and gently toss. Serve at room temperature.

SPROUT SWAP
Sprouted barley or spelt can be used in place of the sprouted wheat berries.

Sprouting time...

Wheat berries
Soak 8–12 hours
Sprout 1-2 days

Hearty and colorful, this salad can be a meal on its own. Use the sprouted grains of your choice, such as wheat berries, spelt, and rye.

SPROUTED GRAIN SALAD
with ROASTED SQUASH and CRANBERRIES

SERVES 6

1 small acorn squash, well scrubbed and dried

4 tbsp extra virgin olive oil + extra for roasting

salt and freshly ground pepper

4 cups sprouted mixed grains

2 tbsp lemon juice

2 large handfuls of baby arugula, roughly chopped

2 tbsp roughly chopped flat-leaf parsley

2 tbsp sprouted pumpkin seeds

2 tbsp sprouted sunflower seeds

⅓ cup dried cranberries, chopped

¼ cup raw hazelnuts, roughly chopped and toasted

¼ cup crumbled goat cheese

PREP 20 MINUTES   **COOK** 20 MINUTES

1 Preheat the oven to 425°F (210°C). Trim each end of the acorn squash, halve and deseed it, and cut it into 16 wedges with the skin intact. Place the squash on a baking sheet and drizzle with a little olive oil, tossing to coat, and then sprinkle with salt and pepper. Place on the top rack and cook for 20 minutes, turning halfway through, until golden brown and soft. Remove from the oven and cool, then halve each piece.

2 Place the sprouted grain mix in a medium heavy-bottomed saucepan and cover with cold water. Bring to a boil, then reduce to a simmer and cook, uncovered, for 15 minutes until tender. Drain and rinse the grains, and then dry them very well.

3 Dress the cooked grains with the olive oil and lemon juice, season with salt and pepper to taste, and toss to combine. Add the arugula, parsley, sprouted seeds, cranberries, and hazelnuts, and toss to combine thoroughly. Mix in the roasted squash pieces and then gently mix through the crumbled goat cheese. Serve at room temperature.

Sprouting time...

Mixed grains
Soak 8-12 hours
Sprout 2 days

Pumpkin and sunflower seeds
Soak 2-3 hours
Sprout 1 day

These toasts pair the smooth, creamy texture of avocado with sharp pickles and earthy sprouts for a simple and satisfying meal.

AVOCADO TOASTS
with PICKLED RADISH *and* SPROUTS

MAKES 2

2 thick slices rye or other whole wheat bread

1 large ripe avocado

squeeze of lime juice

salt and freshly ground pepper

2 scallions, thinly sliced

1 tbsp sprouted pumpkin seeds

handful of broccoli sprouts

PICKLED RADISH

½ cup rice wine vinegar

¼ cup sugar

1 tsp fine sea salt

4 watermelon radishes, washed, trimmed, and thinly sliced

PREP 10 MINUTES, PLUS 1 HOUR FOR PICKLING

1 To make pickled radishes, whisk together the vinegar, sugar, and salt in a small bowl until the sugar has dissolved. Pack the radishes into a small lidded mason jar, pour the vinegar mixture over them until completely covered, and seal. Refrigerate for at least 1 hour before using. (These will keep in the refrigerator for up to 1 week.)

2 Toast the slices of bread. While bread is toasting, make the avocado topping. Roughly chop the avocado and place in a shallow bowl. Squeeze a little lime juice over it, season with salt and pepper, and mash it roughly with the back of a fork. Mix in the scallions and sprouted pumpkin seeds.

3 When the toast is ready, spread the avocado topping over each piece, and add a few slices of pickled radish. Top each toast with broccoli sprouts and serve immediately.

Sprouting time...

Pumpkin seeds
Soak 2-3 hours
Sprout 3 days

Broccoli seeds
Soak 8-12 hours
Sprout 3-5 days

SPROUT SWAP
Give your toasts more heat by replacing the broccoli sprouts with radish sprouts.

This vegetable pancake is inspired by okonomyaki, a popular Japanese street food. Prepare the sprout salad with fresh herbs of your choice.

SAVORY CABBAGE PANCAKES
with FETA and SPROUT SALAD

MAKES 4

PREP 10 MINUTES   **COOK** 15 MINUTES

⅓ cup all-purpose flour

¼ tsp baking powder

salt and freshly ground pepper

1 large egg

⅓ cup vegetable stock

2 heaped cups de-ribbed and finely sliced savoy cabbage

1 cup sprouted mung beans

4 spring onions, finely sliced

2 tbsp finely chopped dill

butter, for frying

1 tbsp olive oil + extra for frying

2 cups mixed mustard, clover, and alfalfa sprouts

handful of mixed herbs, chopped

½ tbsp lemon juice

salt and freshly ground pepper

½ cup crumbled feta cheese

1 In a large bowl, whisk together the flour and baking powder with a pinch of salt and pepper. Add the egg and then the vegetable stock, a little at a time, whisking constantly to produce a smooth, thick batter. Add the cabbage, mung beans, spring onions, and dill, and mix until completely combined.

2 In a non-stick frying pan, heat a bit of butter and olive oil over medium heat until the butter sizzles. Scoop ¼ of the batter into the pan and use a spatula to press it into a firm, even pancake. Cook over medium-low heat for 3–4 minutes.

3 When the underside is brown and crispy, slide the pancake onto a plate. Add more butter and oil to the pan and carefully flip the pancake back into the pan to cook the other side for 3–4 minutes. Keep the pancake warm while you make 3 more, using the same process.

4 Toss the sprouts with the herbs, dress with lemon juice and olive oil, and season with salt and pepper. Gently mix in feta. Serve pancakes immediately, topped with sprout salad.

Sprouting time... }

Mung beans
Soak 8-12 hours
Sprout 3 days

Mustard, clover, and alfalfa seeds
Soak 8-12 hours
Sprout 4-5 days

Mix it up!
BEANS to **SPROUT** TOGETHER

Why sprout a single variety of bean when you can sprout several at once? This hearty mix of colorful legumes can be sprouted together for a flavorful bean burger or a deliciously nutritious addition to soups.

SOAK 8 HOURS   **SPROUT** 2 DAYS

Adzuki beans
With their distinctive burgundy color and light, almost sweet flavor, adzuki beans provide an attractive complement to the other beans in this mix.

Chickpeas
Mild and meaty chickpeas sprout easily and can be used in a wide range of dishes, making them a great choice for mixing with other bean varieties.

Black beans
These small, shiny beans add vibrant color and a creamy texture to the mix. Their earthy flavor pairs well with the nuttier mung beans and adzuki beans.

Mung beans
Little, green mung beans have a firm texture and nutty flavor. They produce a thick, white sprout if grown for several days, but a shorter sprouting time is best for cooking.

Colorful sprouts make a fresh and flavorful filling for these delicate summer rolls. For a more substantial roll, add cooked shrimp.

SPROUTED SUMMER ROLLS
with CHILE-LIME DIPPING SAUCE

MAKES 8

PREP 20 MINUTES

½ mild red chile, finely chopped

½ garlic clove, very finely sliced

2 tbsp rice wine vinegar

1 tbsp lime juice

1 tbsp sugar

1 tsp fine sea salt

1oz (30g) cellophane noodles

8 6-in (15cm) rice paper wrappers

1 carrot, peeled and julienned into 2-in (5cm) pieces

2-in (5cm) segment English cucumber, quartered, deseeded, and finely julienned

handful of radish sprouts

handful of mustard sprouts

½oz (15g) pea shoots

large handful of mixed mint, cilantro, and Thai basil leaves, roughly chopped

1 To make the chile-lime dipping sauce, whisk together the chile, garlic, vinegar, lime juice, sugar, and salt with 3 tablespoons warm water. Set aside. To make the cellophane noodles, place them in a bowl and cover them with just boiled water. Let sit for 5 minutes, then drain and dry thoroughly.

2 Soak 1 rice paper wrapper in a bowl of warm water for 10–15 seconds. Once soft, place wrapper on a clean, damp tea towel. On the bottom third of the paper, make a rectangular pile of 1 tablespoon of the noodles and equal quantities of the vegetables, sprouts, and shoots, leaving ½ inch (1cm) of space on each side. Top with a sprinkle of chopped herbs.

3 Lift the bottom edge of the rice paper and fold it over the filling. Tightly tuck the sides in and over the edges of the filling, then roll up the summer roll, keeping the filling tucked in.

4 Place the roll seam-side down on a serving plate and cover with a second clean, damp tea towel. Continue to make the rolls until all the filling is used up. When you have made the last roll, serve immediately with the dipping sauce alongside.

Sprouting time...

Radish seeds
Soak 8–12 hours
Sprout 4–5 days

Mustard seeds
Soak 8–12 hours
Sprout 4–5 days

Gluten Free

A classic Italian dish gets a healthy twist with sprouted pulses. Just-sprouted beans, with very small shoots, are best for this soup.

WHITE BEAN SOUP
with KALE and PARMESAN

SERVES 4

PREP 10 MINUTES   **COOK** 1 HOUR

3 tbsp olive oil

1 medium white onion, finely chopped

1 celery stalk, de-ribbed and finely chopped

2 carrots, finely chopped

2 garlic cloves, finely chopped

5 cups vegetable stock

1 cup sprouted navy beans

1 cup sprouted cannellini beans

1 sprig rosemary

freshly ground pepper

2 cups de-ribbed and finely shredded kale

salt

4 tbsp freshly grated Parmesan + extra to serve

1 In a Dutch oven or large heavy-bottomed pot, heat the oil over medium heat. Add the onion and cook for 3 minutes, until it is softened but not brown. Add the celery and carrot and cook for another 3 minutes, then add the garlic and cook for 2 minutes more.

2 Add the vegetable stock and bring to a boil. Add the sprouted beans and the rosemary and season well with black pepper. (Do not add salt until beans have cooked.) Bring the soup to a boil then reduce to a simmer and cook, covered, for 45 minutes until the beans are just tender. Remove the rosemary stem.

3 Stir in the shredded kale and cook for another 3–5 minutes, until the kale has wilted and is cooked through. Taste and add salt if necessary. Remove the soup from the heat and stir in the freshly grated Parmesan. Serve immediately with extra grated Parmesan to sprinkle on top.

Gluten Free

Sprouting time...

Navy beans
Soak 8-12 hours
Sprout 3 days

Cannellini beans
Soak 8-12 hours
Sprout 3 days

This fragrant curry pairs dark, nutty adzuki beans with hearty mushrooms and creamy coconut milk.

ADZUKI BEAN CURRY
with SPINACH *and* MUSHROOMS

SERVES 4

PREP 10 MINUTES   **COOK** 1¼ HOURS

2 cups sprouted adzuki beans

3 tbsp coconut oil

1 medium white onion, finely chopped

2 garlic cloves, crushed

2-in (5cm) piece fresh ginger, peeled and grated

8oz (225g) cremini mushrooms, cleaned, trimmed, and quartered

1 heaped tbsp curry powder

13.5oz (400ml) can coconut milk

2 cups vegetable stock

4oz (115g) baby spinach

salt and freshly ground pepper

1 Place sprouted adzuki beans in a medium heavy-bottomed saucepan. Cover well with cold water and bring to a boil. Reduce to a simmer and cook, uncovered, for 20 minutes until they are partially cooked and beginning to soften. Drain.

2 In a large skillet with a lid, heat coconut oil over medium heat. Add the onion and cook for 3 minutes, until soft but not brown. Add the garlic and ginger and cook for another minute, then add the mushrooms and cook for 5 more minutes, until they start to color. Finally, turn the heat to low and stir the curry powder into the vegetables. Cook for a minute more, stirring constantly.

3 Stir in the coconut milk and vegetable stock. Add the adzuki beans and bring the mixture to a boil, then reduce to a simmer and cook, covered, for 40 minutes or until beans are soft.

4 Remove the lid, turn up the heat, and stir in the spinach a handful at a time until wilted, about 2–3 minutes. Season to taste with salt and pepper and serve immediately.

Gluten Free

Sprouting time...
Adzuki beans
Soak 8-12 hours
Sprout 4 days

This light and refreshing salad pairs crisp spirals of cucumber and zucchini with the bold flavors of ginger, garlic, and sesame.

ASIAN STYLE SALAD
with SPROUTED MUNG BEANS and MINT

SERVES 2

2 tbsp rice wine vinegar

2 tsp sugar

1 tsp sesame oil

½ tsp soy sauce

¼ tsp finely grated ginger

¼ tsp finely grated garlic

½ medium zucchini, spiralized

3-in (8cm) segment English cucumber, spiralized

1oz (30g) sprouted mung beans

1oz (30g) pea shoots

a few thin slices of red onion, to taste

2 tbsp roughly chopped mint leaves

1 tbsp roughly chopped salted peanuts

PREP 10 MINUTES

1 To make the dressing, combine the vinegar, sugar, sesame oil, soy sauce, ginger, and garlic in a small bowl. Whisk until the sugar has dissolved.

2 Place the zucchini, cucumber, sprouted mung beans, pea shoots, red onion, and mint in a serving bowl. Pour the dressing over top and toss until salad is well coated, taking care to pile the salad into the center of the bowl.

3 Sprinkle with the chopped peanuts and a few extra mint leaves if desired, and serve immediately.

"Mung beans contain peptides that may help lower blood pressure"

Gluten Free

Sprouting time... } **Mung beans**
Soak 8-12 hours
Sprout 3 days

SPROUT SWAP
For more crunch, sprouted green peas can take the place of pea shoots.

Briny seaweed flakes and nutty sprouted seeds add flavor and texture to the sprouted brown rice base in this satisfying and nutritious dish.

BROWN RICE SUSHI BOWL
with SPROUTED SEEDS *and* PICKLED RADISH

SERVES 1

PREP 15 MINUTES   **COOK** 20 MINUTES

1 cup sprouted short grain brown rice

1 tbsp rice wine vinegar

¼ tsp sugar

¼ tsp salt

1 tbsp sprouted pumpkin seeds

1 tbsp sprouted sunflower seeds

1 tbsp sprouted sesame seeds

0.17oz (5g) packet dried seaweed snack sheets

1-in (2.5cm) segment English cucumber, halved, deseeded, and finely sliced

½ small avocado, sliced

a few slices of pickled watermelon radish (see p44)

1 Place the sprouted brown rice in a medium heavy-bottomed saucepan and cover with 1 cup of cold water. Bring to a boil, reduce to a simmer and cook, covered, for 15–20 minutes, until all the water has evaporated and the rice is nearly tender.

2 Put the rice wine vinegar, sugar, and salt in a small saucepan and heat, whisking constantly, until the sugar is just dissolved. Mix the dressing into the rice and let sit, covered, for 5 minutes.

3 Mix the sprouted pumpkin seeds, sunflower seeds, and sesame seeds into the warm rice. Set aside 1 or 2 of the seaweed sheets and crumble the rest over the rice. Mix well to combine.

4 Turn the warm rice mixture into a serving bowl and top it with sliced cucumber, sliced avocado, and a few pickled radish slices. Crumble the remaining seaweed sheets over top before serving.

Sprouting time...

Brown rice
Soak 12–18 hours
Sprout 2 days

Sesame seeds
Soak 2–8 hours
Sprout 1–3 days

Sunflower and pumpkin seeds
Soak 2–3 hours
Sprout: 1–2 days

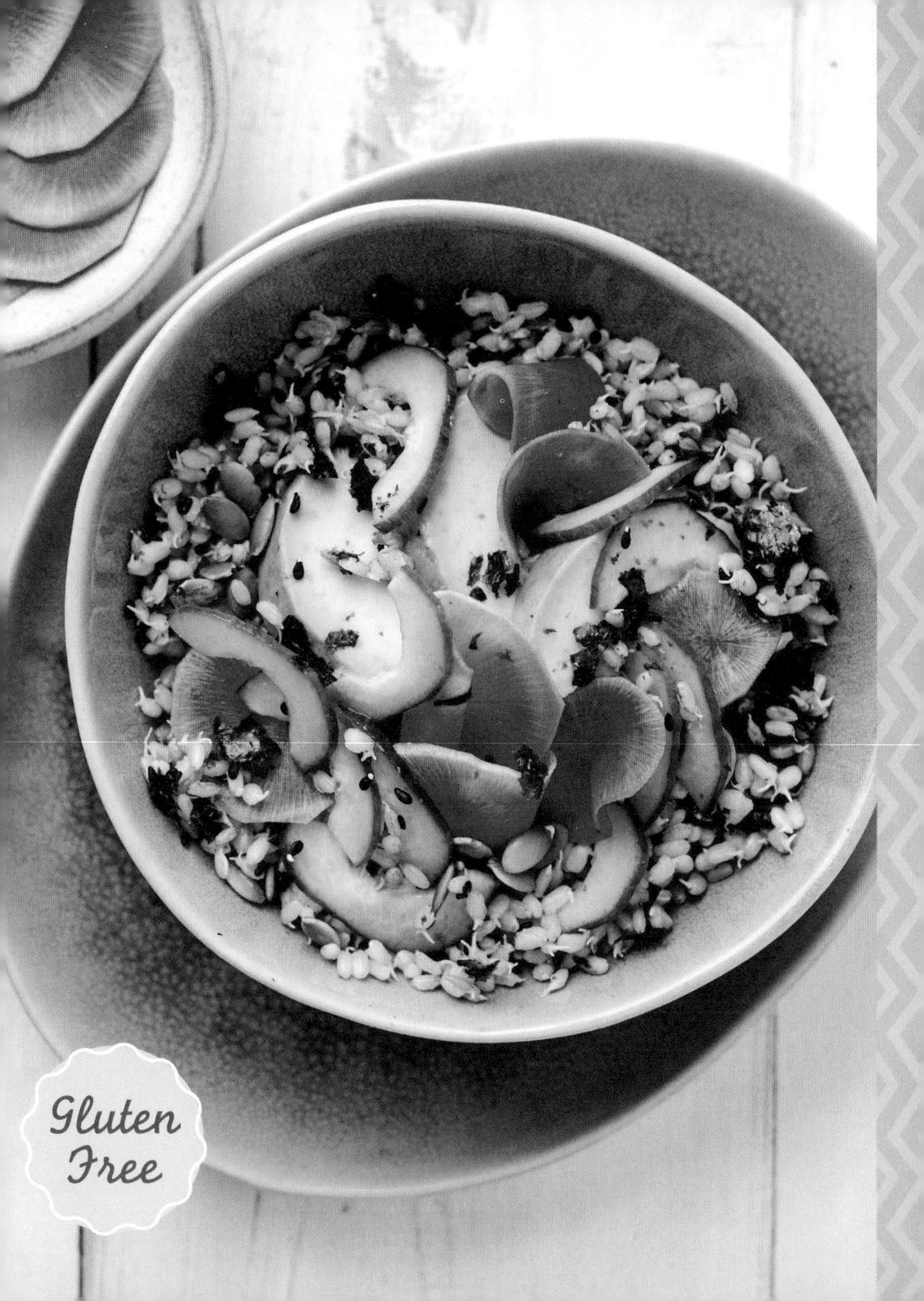
Gluten Free

Mix it up!
GRAINS to **SPROUT** TOGETHER

Grains with similar sprouting times can be sprouted together in one jar. Try this mix of whole grains for an added dimension of flavor and texture to your pilafs, hot cereals, and grain salads.

SOAK 6 HOURS **SPROUT** 2 DAYS

Barley
Look for hulless barley, which does not need to be stripped of its hull, making it ideal for sprouting. Barley has a mild flavor and pleasant chewiness that complements the other grains in this mix.

Buckwheat
Buckwheat groats are the hulled seeds of the buckwheat plant. These soft and tender kernels contrast with the chewier grains for textural variety.

Wheat berries
Sweet, nutty wheat berries have a full, robust flavor and a firm texture. In addition to being an excellent source of fiber, they have the highest protein content of any wheat-derived grain.

Oats
Hulless oats, which are grown without a hull, are mild and slightly chewy. Not just for breakfast, sprouted oats are delicious in grain salads.

These hearty burgers can be made with any type of firm sprouted legume, such as lentils, navy beans, or pinto beans.

SPROUTED BEAN BURGERS
with RAW CASHEW MAYO

SERVES 4

3 cups sprouted mixed beans

4 tbsp grapeseed oil

1 cup finely diced cremini mushrooms

1½ cups fresh white breadcrumbs

½ small onion, finely grated

2 tbsp finely chopped flat-leaf parsley

2 tsp Worcestershire sauce

1 large egg, beaten

salt and freshly ground pepper

1 cup raw cashews, soaked for 3 hours

2 tbsp lemon juice

1 tbsp olive oil

1 small garlic clove, crushed

TO SERVE

4 hamburger buns

sliced avocado and tomato

handful of alfalfa sprouts

PREP 15 MINUTES, PLUS 1 HOUR TO CHILL   **COOK** 1 HOUR

1 Place the beans in a saucepan of cold water and bring to a boil. Reduce to a simmer and cook for 35–40 minutes until they are soft. Drain and rinse the beans then set aside to cool.

2 In a non-stick frying pan, heat 2 tablespoons oil over medium heat. Add the mushrooms and cook for 5–7 minutes, until they are cooked through. Set aside to cool.

3 Put the beans and all the other ingredients, apart from the remaining oil, into a food processor and season with salt and pepper. Pulse the mixture until it is just mixed but still has some texture. With damp hands, shape the mixture into 4 patties and chill, covered, for 1 hour.

4 To make the cashew mayo, drain the cashews and place them in a food processor with lemon juice, olive oil, garlic, and 5–6 tablespoons water. Process until smooth and chill until needed.

5 In a large non-stick frying pan, heat the remaining 2 tablespoons oil over medium heat. Cook the burger patties for 3–4 minutes on each side, until well browned and cooked through. Serve immediately on toasted buns, topped with avocado, tomato, alfalfa sprouts, and cashew mayo.

Sprouting time...

Mixed beans
Soak 8–12 hours
Sprout 3 days

Sprouted chickpeas cook quickly and produce a smooth, fresh-tasting hummus that is enhanced by the zesty cilantro topping.

SPROUTED HUMMUS
with LEMON *and* CILANTRO

SERVES 4

2 cups sprouted chickpeas
2 tbsp tahini
4 tbsp lemon juice
2 garlic cloves, crushed
1 scant cup extra virgin olive oil
salt and freshly ground pepper
pita wedges, to serve

TOPPING

1 cup loosely packed cilantro leaves, about ½ bunch
¼ cup extra virgin olive oil
finely grated zest of 1 lemon

PREP 10 MINUTES **COOK** 20-25 MINUTES

1 To make hummus, place the chickpeas in a medium heavy-bottomed saucepan and cover with cold water. Bring to a boil over high heat, skim any foam from the surface, and reduce to a simmer. Cook, uncovered, for 20–25 minutes until the chickpeas are soft. Drain and cool the chickpeas, and peel them if you prefer. (This makes for an even smoother texture.)

2 Place the chickpeas, tahini, lemon juice, garlic, and most of the olive oil in a food processor and season with salt and pepper. Process the mixture to a smooth paste, drizzling in the rest of the oil a little at a time with the motor running until you reach a smooth consistency. Finally, add 1 tablespoon cold water and process again until it is completely smooth.

3 To make cilantro topping, place all the ingredients in a small food processor bowl and process until nearly smooth. When ready to eat, scoop the hummus out into a serving bowl, make a depression in the middle, and swirl the topping onto the hummus. Serve with pita wedges alongside.

Sprouting time... }

Chickpeas
Soak 8-12 hours
Sprout 3 days

Warm smoked paprika and spicy jalapeño bring the flavors of the southwest to this hearty quesadilla.

BLACK BEAN QUESADILLA
with SWEET POTATO and PAPRIKA

MAKES 6

PREP 10 MINUTES   **COOK** 40 MINUTES

2 cups sprouted black beans

1 large sweet potato, peeled and diced

6 scallions, trimmed and finely chopped

¼ cup sweet corn

½ jalapeño, deseeded and very finely chopped

¼ cup finely chopped fresh cilantro leaves

¾ tsp smoked paprika

salt and freshly ground pepper

1 heaped cup grated cheese, such as Cheddar

olive oil, for frying

12 6-in (15cm) soft corn or flour tortillas

1 Place the beans in a saucepan of cold water and bring to a boil. Reduce to a simmer and cook, uncovered, for 30 minutes until soft. Drain and rinse the beans then set aside to cool.

2 Place the sweet potato in a saucepan and cover with plenty of water. Bring to a boil, then reduce the heat and cook, uncovered, for 15–20 minutes until soft. Drain the cooking water.

3 Place the black beans in a flat-bottomed dish and mash until they are partially broken up. Add the sweet potato and continue to mash until it is broken down. Add the scallions, sweet corn, jalapeño, cilantro, and smoked paprika and mix well. Season with salt and pepper and mix in half of the cheese.

4 In a large non-stick frying pan, heat a little olive oil over medium heat. Spread ⅙ of the bean mixture over a tortilla, cover it with ⅙ of the remaining cheese, and top with a second tortilla. Cook for 2–3 minutes on each side until it is golden brown all over. Repeat to cook remaining quesadillas. Serve immediately.

Sprouting time... }

Black beans
Soak 8–12 hours
Sprout 3 days

The flavors of ginger, garlic, and sesame infuse this Asian-inspired dish, which comes together quickly, making it an easy weeknight meal.

VEGETABLE STIR-FRY
with SPROUTED QUINOA *and* SESAME

SERVES 2

2 tbsp canola oil

2 tsp sesame oil

1 medium carrot, peeled and finely julienned

¼ medium red onion, finely sliced

½ medium zucchini, finely julienned

1 cup sprouted mung beans

1 cup finely shredded savoy cabbage

2 tbsp peeled and finely chopped ginger

2 garlic cloves, minced

1 jalapeño, deseeded and finely chopped

3 cups sprouted quinoa

2 tbsp sprouted sesame seeds

2 tbsp reduced-sodium soy sauce

PREP 10 MINUTES   **COOK** 5 MINUTES

1 Heat a wok or large frying pan over a high heat and add the canola and sesame oils. When the oil has almost begun to smoke, add the carrots, and stir-fry for 1 minute. Add the onion and zucchini and cook for another minute. Add the sprouted mung beans, cabbage, ginger, garlic, and jalapeño and cook for a minute more.

2 Add the sprouted quinoa and sesame seeds to the vegetables, and cook over a high heat, turning constantly, until the quinoa begins to brown, about 2 minutes. Add the soy sauce to the pan and cook for a final minute before serving immediately.

Sprouting time... }

Mung beans
Soak 8–12 hours
Sprout 3 days

Quinoa
Soak 30 minutes
Sprout 2 days

Sesame seeds
Soak 6 hours
Sprout 3 days

This earthy, cool-weather stew brings together the nuttiness of sprouted barley and the sweetness of root vegetables.

ROOT VEGETABLE STEW
with SPROUTED BARLEY *and* SORGHUM

SERVES 4

4 tbsp olive oil

2 cups diced young turnips

2 cups diced carrots

2 cups diced parsnips

1 medium yellow onion, finely diced

2 celery stalks, trimmed, de-ribbed, and finely diced

1 cup sprouted barley

1 cup sorghum

2 quarts (2l) vegetable stock

1 tsp chopped fresh thyme leaves

salt and freshly ground pepper

¼ cup finely chopped flat-leaf parsley

PREP 10 MINUTES   **COOK** 1 HOUR 10 MINUTES

1 In a Dutch oven or large heavy-bottomed pot with a lid, heat the olive oil over medium heat. Add the turnips, carrots, and parsnips and cook for 5 minutes, turning occasionally, until they begin to brown. Remove them from the pan and set aside.

2 Add the onion and celery and cook over medium heat for 3 minutes until they start to soften, but do not brown. Add the barley and sorghum and cook for another 2 minutes until the grains start to color.

3 Add the vegetable stock and fresh thyme, and season well with salt and pepper. Bring to a boil, reduce to a simmer, and cook, covered, for 40 minutes until the grains are partially cooked.

4 Remove the lid and turn up the heat. Add the browned root vegetables and parsley to the pan and bring back to a boil. Reduce to a simmer and cook, uncovered, for a final 20 minutes until the vegetables have softened and the stock has reduced. Season with salt and pepper if needed and serve immediately.

⚠ *Sorghum is nutritious when cooked, but should not be sprouted. Prolonged soaking activates chemicals stored within the grain and makes it potentially toxic.*

Sprouting time... } **Barley**
Soak 6–12 hours
Sprout 2 days

"Barley's high fiber content can help lower cholesterol"

INDEX